RAISING THE BAR

Black Women Who Changed Gymnastics

Ngeri Nnachi

Cicely Lewis, Executive Editor

Lerner Publications ◆ Minneapolis

LETTER FROM CICELY LEWIS

Dear Reader,

When you think of today's star Black athletes, who comes to mind? Maybe you think of LeBron James, Mookie Betts, Dak Prescott, or Simone Biles. They are all great athletes. But do you know who paved the way for them?

Cicely Lewis

I began Read Woke Books to challenge social norms and to share stories of people from underrepresented and oppressed groups. In this series, you will be introduced to lesser-known athletes and the barriers they overcame to make great changes in sports.

Sports is more than a game. Throughout history, sports have been a way to help fight injustices in our world. As you read, think about how the actions athletes have made in their sports have impacted the world.

I hope these books inspire you to never give up. Someone has to take the first step, and it might as well be you.

Power to the Reader,

Cicely Lewis, Executive Editor

TABLE OF CONTENTS

Luci Collins (*third from left*) and the other members of the 1980 US women's Olympics gymnastics team meeting with Nancy Reagan at the White House in 1981

AN OLYMPIC FIRST

In 1980 gymnasts from around the country competed at the US Olympic Trials. They hoped to be chosen for the team going to the Olympics. That year 16-year-old Luci Collins made history. She became the first Black woman chosen for a US Olympic gymnastics team.

The 1980 Olympic Games were held in the Soviet Union, then a nation of 15 countries that included Russia. The US boycotted the 1980 Olympics to protest the Soviet Union for invading Afghanistan in 1979. Collins never had the chance to compete in the Olympics because of the boycott.

"My one chance to compete on the Olympic stage had passed me by," Collins said. "I do still wonder what if?"

Gymnastics has been around for decades. But racism kept Black women out of the sport for a long time. Black women such as Collins, Gabby Douglas, Konnor McClain, and Simone Biles have worked hard to make great firsts in the sport.

In 2012 Gabby Douglas becomes the first Black American to win the individual all-around.

Gymnasts of Team Yugoslavia (*left*) and Team Poland (*right*) at the 1936 Olympics

CHAPTER 1

A GROWING SPORT

The best US gymnasts compete at the Olympics, World Championships, and US National Championships. At first, only men could compete at the events. When women started competing, racist ideas and beliefs kept Black women out of the sport.

In 1883 the Amateur Athletic Union became the first group to grow amateur sports in the US, including artistic gymnastics. Gymnasts competed in the union's first championships in 1897. It was held every year until 1971.

The first World Championships was held in 1903. Gymnasts competed at it every two years until 1991. Since then, gymnasts have competed at it every year.

Olympic gymnastics opened to women in 1928. Four years later, the first US women's team formed. The team was made up of only white women.

But women's gymnastics was still not well known, so it was dropped from the 1932 Olympics. After the 1932 Olympics, a group formed to grow the sport for women. Women gymnasts competed in all the Summer Olympics beginning in 1936.

A Czechoslovakian gymnast trains for the 1936 Olympics.

The US women's team went to the 1936 Olympics in Berlin, Germany. Women only competed in the team all-around event. In 1952 the Olympics included individual events for women. They competed in the vault, uneven bars, balance beam, and floor exercise events.

Alice Coachman (*center*), the 1948 women's high jump gold medalist, was the first Black woman to win a gold medal in the Olympics. Consider why Black American women were able to compete in Olympic sports other than gymnastics in 1948.

Cathy Rigby of Team USA during the floor exercise event at the 1968 Olympics

In 1963 USA Gymnastics formed. This group is in charge of the sport in the US. The first US Gymnastics Championships was held that year. Gymnasts compete at the championships every year.

The Amateur Sports Act passed in 1978. It created the US Olympic Committee, which formed groups in charge of each Olympic sport.

DID YOU KNOW?

In 1983 Dianne Durham became the first Black woman to win the US Gymnastics Championships all-around. After Durham stopped competing, she became a gymnastics judge and coach.

Dianne Durham (*right*) signs autographs after winning the 1983 US Gymnastics Championships.

Durham in the uneven bars event at the 1983 US Gymnastics Championships

Women gymnasts had more ways to compete in the sport. But US Olympic gymnastics teams were only made up of white women until 1992. In the 1990s, artistic gymnastics changed forever.

REFLECT

Consider why Black women and other women of color didn't compete on the US gymnastics team at the Olympics until 1992. What may have stopped them from joining higher levels of the sport?

Betty Okino performs on the balance beam at the 1992 World Championships.

CHAPTER 2
BREAKING GROUND

Young Black women are a force in gymnastics. They are doing things that many have not seen before. They lead the way for others in the sport.

In 1991 Betty Okino became the first Black woman to win multiple World Championships medals. Then, in 1992, Okino and Dominique Dawes became the first Black women gymnasts to compete in the Olympics. They helped Team USA win the bronze medal.

In 1995 Dawes won all the events at the US Gymnastics

Championships. She was the first woman to win all the events since 1969. The following year, Dawes and Team USA won their first Olympic team gold medal. At the 2000 Olympics, Dawes became the first Black woman to win an individual Olympic medal and to win gold in the sport.

Dominique Dawes competing at the 1996 Olympics

Gabby Douglas competing in the balance beam event at the 2012 Olympics

At the 2012 Olympics, Gabby Douglas became the first American gymnast to win gold medals in both the team and individual all-around. Douglas was also the first Black American to win the all-around. Then she helped Team USA win gold at the 2016 Olympics.

"I'm so thrilled to change my website and take down the fact that I was the only African American with a gold medal."

—Dominique Dawes, on Gabby Douglas winning the individual all-around gold, 2012

Simone Biles was on the 2016 US Olympic team with Douglas. Biles went home with five medals. Four of them were gold, making her the gymnast with the most gold medal wins at a single Olympics. She also helped Team USA win the silver medal at the 2020 Olympics in Tokyo, which was held in 2021 due to the spread of the disease COVID-19.

In 2023 Biles won the all-around for the sixth time at the World Championships. Biles has the most medals of any gymnast in history with a combined 34 Olympic and World Championships medals.

Simone Biles holds up her bronze medal for the balance beam event at the Tokyo Olympics.

Left to right: Shilese Jones, Konnor McClain, and Jordan Chiles finished in the top three for the 2022 US Gymnastics Championships individual all-around.

At the 2022 US Gymnastics Championships, Konnor McClain, Shilese Jones, and Jordan Chiles earned the top three spots in the individual all-around. They made history as the first three Black female gymnasts to take all three spots on the podium. McClain won gold, Jones won silver, and Chiles won bronze.

REFLECT

What steps could be taken to improve diversity in gymnastics? Why is this important?

DID YOU KNOW?

Betty Okino joined the USA Gymnastics Hall of Fame in 2002. Dawes joined in 2005, Douglas joined in 2017, and Durham joined in 2021.

Douglas competing in the uneven bars event at the 2012 Olympics

Fisk University head coach Corrinne Tarver speaks with gymnast Liberty Mora at a meet in 2023.

CHAPTER 3

COLLEGE COACHES AND STARS

Elite level competitions are an important part of gymnastics. But Black women are also breaking ground as coaches and athletes in college gymnastics.

In 1984, 13-year-old Dionne Foster became the first elite gymnast in Alabama. She later went to college at the University of Alabama. There, she became a 17-time All-American.

Corrinne Tarver was a student at the University of Georgia. In 1989 she became the first Black gymnast to win

Corrinne Tarver

Ashley Miles in 2004

the National Collegiate Athletics Association (NCAA) all-around.

Ashley Miles also went to the University of Alabama. In 2004 she became the first Alabama gymnast to win two NCAA titles in a season. The following season, she won seven all-around, 10 vault, and nine floor exercise titles.

Miles was a 12-time All-American. She became the head gymnastics coach at Iowa State University in 2023.

Kelsey Hinton dreamed of becoming a head coach in Division 1. It is the highest level of college sports in the NCAA. The US has 62 Division 1 gymnastics teams.

Hinton was an assistant coach at William & Mary until 2019. Then she became the head coach. She was the first Black head gymnastics coach

Kelsey Hinton coaching gymnasts

at the school. Hinton became the second Black woman head coach in Division 1.

Historically Black colleges and universities (HBCUs) formed before 1964. Their main mission is to teach Black Americans. Fisk University formed the first HBCU women's gymnastics team in 2022. Tarver became the team's first coach.

Talladega College formed a women's team in 2023. Aja Sims-Fletcher became the coach and the second gymnastics coach at an HBCU.

Sloane Blakely competing at a 2023 NCAA gymnastics meet

Sloane Blakely was a member of the US national team in the 2018–2019 season. She began college at the University of Florida in 2022. She was named an All-American in 2023.

DID YOU KNOW?

Blakely's younger sister, Skye, is also an elite gymnast. Skye Blakely helped Team USA win gold at the 2022 and 2023 World Championships.

Trinity Thomas receives a perfect 10 for her uneven bars routine in 2023.

Trinity Thomas won the NCAA all-around in 2022. In 2023 she earned her 28th perfect 10. She tied for most perfect 10s in NCAA history.

REFLECT

Why should gymnastics and other sports include athletes and coaches of all races and abilities? How does representation affect young athletes?

Left to right: Biles, McKayla Maroney, and Aly Raisman are among the gymnasts testifying in 2021 about the abuse they faced while competing for USA Gymnastics.

CHAPTER 4
MAKING CHANGE

On and off the mat, Black gymnasts are speaking out for the issues they care about. People are also working to get more diversity in the sport. They are paying more attention to the safety of athletes.

Over 200 gymnasts including Biles and Douglas have spoken out against abuse they faced while competing for USA Gymnastics. Courts have found that the group failed to protect these athletes.

Biles flips on the balance beam at the Tokyo Olympics.

USA Gymnastics has since been working to better protect the physical and mental health of gymnasts. They have changed their group's leaders and have created an Athlete Bill of Rights. The bill lists ways athletes are protected.

In 2021 Biles got the twisties at the Olympics in Tokyo, Japan. When a gymnast has the twisties, they lose their sense of space in the air. This might cause gymnasts to land unsafely and get hurt.

Biles decided to protect her health by removing herself from two events at the Tokyo Olympics. She has spoken about mental health as well as social justice.

"I say put mental health first. . . . It's okay sometimes to even sit out the big competitions to focus on yourself because it shows how strong of a competitor or a person that you really are."

—Simone Biles

Some groups are working to get more Black girls and other girls of color in the sport. Coach Derrin Moore started Brown Girls Do Gymnastics in 2015. The group provides support, classes, and training to gymnasts.

Derrin Moore (*left*) of Brown Girls Do Gymnastics coaching a gymnast

Wendy Hilliard attends an event put on by the Women's Sports Foundation in 2023.

Hall of Famer Wendy Hilliard created the Wendy Hilliard Gymnastics Foundation in 1996. It provides free and low-cost classes to over 20,000 youth in Harlem, New York, and Detroit, Michigan.

REFLECT

Some gymnasts and other athletes speak out about issues such as social justice. What issues are important to you? How can you make a difference?

DID YOU KNOW?

In rhythmic gymnastics, gymnasts perform a dancelike floor routine. They may use hoops and ribbons. The first Rhythmic Gymnastics World Championships were held in 1963, and the sport was added to the Olympics in 1984. In 1978 Hilliard became the first Black rhythmic gymnast on the US national team.

More than 10 percent of USA Gymnastics members are Black. More Black women are finding success and breaking records in the sport than ever. Young Black girls across the US can see themselves represented by gymnasts and get inspired to make their own change.

Skye Blakely competes in the uneven bars event at the 2023 World Championships.

GLOSSARY

abuse: to hurt or harm by treating badly

all-American: an honor given to one of the best amateur athletes in a sport

all-around: a contest in which an individual or team competes in each gymnastics event. The scores are totaled to determine the winner.

amateur: someone who takes part in an activity or sport without pay

balance beam: gymnastics equipment with a 4-inch-wide (10 cm) beam

boycott: to refuse to buy, use, or go to an event in protest

elite: the top level of a sport or group

floor exercise: an event where gymnasts perform routines in a 40-foot (12 m) square

podium: a structure with three platforms for the athletes that won first, second, or third place to stand on as they receive medals

uneven bars: an event where gymnasts perform on and move between two bars set at different heights

vault: gymnastics equipment that includes a springboard and a vaulting table that gymnasts launch from

SOURCE NOTES

5 "1980 Olympic Gymnastics Team Reflects 30 Years Later," USA Gymnastics, August 16, 2010, https://usagym.org/1980-olympic-gymnastics-team-reflects-30-years-later/.

14 Celisa Calacal and Lindsay Gibbs, "America's Painful Journey from Prejudice to Greatness in Women's Gymnastics," Think Progress, August 8, 2016, https://archive.thinkprogress.org/americas-painful-journey-from-prejudice-to-greatness-in-women-s-gymnastics-a35c8e4eebb7/.

25 Diane J. Cho, "'I Don't Have to Be Fine': Everything Simone Biles Has Said about Mental Health," *People*, updated December 1, 2021, https://people.com/sports/everything-simone-biles-has-said-about-mental-health/.

READ WOKE READING LIST

Adero, Malaika. *A Black Woman Did That*. New York: Downtown Bookworks, 2020.

Brown Girls Do Gymnastics
http://www.browngirlsdogymnastics.com

Meadows, Michelle. *Flying High: The Story of Gymnastics Champion Simone Biles*. New York: Henry Holt, 2020.

Olympics: Gabrielle Douglas
https://olympics.com/en/athletes/gabrielle-douglas

Simone Biles
https://simonebiles.com

Smith, Elliott. *Black Achievements in Sports: Celebrating Fritz Pollard, Simone Biles, and More*. Minneapolis: Lerner Publications, 2024.

Team USA: Black Excellence All-Around
https://www.teamusa.com/news/2023/february/28/black-excellence-all-around

USA Gymnastics Hall of Fame
https://usagym.org/halloffame/

INDEX

PHOTO ACKNOWLEDGMENTS

Image credits: Cicely Lewis portrait photo by Fernando Decillis, p. 2; Courtesy Ronald Reagan Library, p. 4; Al Tielemans/Getty Images, p. 5; Paul Popper/Popperfoto/Getty Images, p. 6; Roger Viollet/Getty Images, p. 7; AP Photo, pp. 8, 9; AP Photo/Lisa Genesen, p. 10; AP Photo/Lennox McLendon, p. 11; Simon Bruty/Getty Images, p. 12; AP Photo/Amy Sancetta, p. 13; THOMAS COEX/Getty Images, p. 14; AP Photo/Jae C. Hong, p. 15; AP Photo/Mike Carlson, p. 16; PCN Photography/Alamy, p. 17; Stew Milne/Getty Images, p. 18; University of Georgia Athletic Association, p. 19 (top); Steve Grayson/Getty Images, p. 19 (bottom); William & Mary Athletics, p. 20; AP Photo/Gary McCullough, p. 21; AP Photo/Kyle Okita/CSM via ZUMA Press Wire, p. 22; AP Photo/Saul Loeb/Pool, p. 23; AP Photo/David McIntyre/ZUMA Press Wire, p. 24; Brown Girls Do Gymnastics, p. 25; Dia Dipasupil/Getty Images, p. 26; AP Photo/Geert vanden Wijngaert, p. 27. Design elements: Sandipkumar Patel/Getty Images; Colors Hunter/Getty Images.

Cover: AP Photo/Kyle Okita/CSM via ZUMA Press Wire; AP Photo/Daniela Porcelli/SPP/Sipa USA.

This book is dedicated to my Zola darling. May you always find inspiration to soar high and be unique. Aunty Geri loves you!

Lerner Publications Company
An imprint of Lerner Publishing Group, Inc.
241 First Avenue North
Minneapolis, MN 55401 USA

For reading levels and more information, look up this title at www.lernerbooks.com.

Main body text set in Aptifer Sans LT Pro.
Typeface provided by Linotype AG.

Editor: Brianna Kaiser **Designer:** Viet Chu **Photo Editor:** Nicole Berglund
Lerner team: Martha Kranes

Library of Congress Cataloging-in-Publication Data

Names: Nnachi, Ngeri, author.
Title: Raising the bar : Black women who changed gymnastics / Ngeri Nnachi.
Description: Minneapolis, MN : Lerner Publications, [2025] | Series: Read woke books. Black trailblazers in sports | Includes bibliographical references and index. | Audience: Ages 9–14 | Audience: Grades 4–6 | Summary: "Black athletes such as Simone Biles have dominated the gymnastics world. But there's also been a lack of diversity in the sport. Learn about Black women who have made a difference in gymnastics"— Provided by publisher.
Identifiers: LCCN 2023038272 (print) | LCCN 2023038273 (ebook) | ISBN 9798765611579 (library binding) | ISBN 9798765628522 (paperback) | ISBN 9798765632765 (epub)
Subjects: LCSH: African American women gymnasts—Biography—Juvenile literature. | Gymnastics—United States—History—Juvenile literature.
Classification: LCC GV460 .N63 2025 (print) | LCC GV460 (ebook) | DDC 796.44092/52—dc23/eng/20230925

LC record available at https://lccn.loc.gov/2023038272
LC ebook record available at https://lccn.loc.gov/2023038273

Manufactured in the United States of America
2-1011774-51779-10/17/2024